PRAISE FOR
the whoopie pie BOOK

"An absolutely gorgeous book by my favorite cake maker in the whole world."
—JAMIE OLIVER

"Claire Ptak creates the very best desserts: Simple, delicious, pure. This is a charming book that perfectly captures its subject." —ALICE WATERS

"Claire has taken store cupboard basics and turned them into a book of recipes so delicious you'll want to eat the pages." —APRIL BLOOMFIELD

"Claire Ptak is my favorite baker. Her competent yet whimsical style imbues everything she bakes—from a classic French apple tart to the humble whoopie pie—with a delicate magic." —DAVID TANIS, author of *A Platter of Figs* and *Heart of the Artichoke*

THE EXPERIMENT BECAUSE EVERY BOOK IS A TEST OF NEW IDEAS

THE EXPERIMENT

NEW YORK

the
whoopie pie
BOOK

60 IRRESISTIBLE RECIPES FOR CAKE SANDWICHES
CLASSIC AND NEW

CLAIRE PTAK

The Experiment, LLC
260 Fifth Avenue
New York, NY 10001–6408
www.theexperimentpublishing.com

Originally published in Great Britain in 2010 in somewhat different form by Square Peg, an imprint of the Random House Group Limited.

Many of the designations used by manufacturers and sellers to distinguish their products are claimed as trademarks. Where those designations appear in this book and The Experiment was aware of a trademark claim, the designations have been capitalized.

The Experiment's books are available at special discounts when purchased in bulk for premiums and sales promotions as well as for fundraising or educational use. For details, contact us at info@theexperimentpublishing.com.

Library of Congress Control Number: 2011930200
ISBN 978-1-61519-039-3
Ebook ISBN 978-1-61519-141-3

Cover design by Susi Oberhelman
Cover and interior photographs by Colin Campbell
Food styling by Claire Ptak | Styling assistant: Adriana Nascimento
Text design by Pauline Neuwirth, Neuwirth & Associates, Inc.

Printed in China
Distributed by Workman Publishing Company, Inc.
First U.S. edition published September 2011
10 9 8 7 6 5 4 3 2 1

for my mom elisabeth

contents

· ·

introduction

. . . .

A WHOOPIE PIE is not a cookie or a typical cake, and it's definitely not a pie. A whoopie pie is somewhere between a cupcake and an ice cream sandwich—a cupcake with the "icing" in the middle. These cake sandwiches are popping up in bakeries and coffee shops everywhere, but many can be dry and heavy. The essence of a good whoopie pie is the soft, tender crumb of the cake and the fluffy, creamy filling. Follow these recipes carefully and you will have wondrous results.

Whoopie pies originated in the United States in the 1920s, though their precise birthplace is still under debate. These cake sandwiches have been showing up in the lunch boxes of the Pennsylvania Amish for generations (the story goes that the Amish farmers' wives made them from leftover cake batter as a lunch treat for their husbands) and bakeries and gas stations in the state of Maine have been selling them for years. They now have an international following, partly because everyone seems to be in search of a new cake to replace the ever-popular cupcake, but mostly because they are just so delicious.

I love individual cakes that are not too fussy. I make and sell cupcakes, cakes, and savory treats at Violet, my East London bakery. When we added whoopie pies to the menu, early skeptics were surprised at how soft and moist they were without being overly sweet. This book will show you how to make them at home using fresh, seasonal ingredients, the way I approach all my baking.

The original whoopie pie combines chocolate cake with a marshmallow filling. Today, most recipes rely on a marshmallow spread from a jar. I've taken that idea and updated it with a completely fresh marshmallow filling made with egg whites, sugar, and golden syrup, which is then sandwiched between rounds of the softest chocolate cake you've ever eaten.

Typically, whoopies are made in 4-inch rounds, just the right size to hold in your hand for eating. I've given instructions for making smaller-sized ones, too—which are perfect for children's tiny fingers, or when you want just a little treat, and great for serving at parties. You'll find plenty of recipes for other whoopie pie bases, too, including pumpkin, strawberry, and mocha, as well as ideas for mouthwatering fillings flavored with fruit purées or enriched with homemade caramel.

Whoopie pies can also be used to make sticky, gooey desserts, and I've included variations on traditional British sweets such as rhubarb and custard and American

favorites such as banana cream pie. Or the pies can be frozen—my personal favorite—as with my oatmeal ice cream sandwich. The last chapter features a selection of other sweet sandwiches, including peanut butter sandwich cookies and an easy macaroon. I also threw in my favorite brownie recipe, and topped it with ice cream, chocolate sauce, and preserved cherries . . . why not?

The Amish are given credit for pioneering the idea of putting the icing or frosting inside the cakes to make them easier to transport in lunch boxes. Schoolchildren and farmers are said to have responded to finding these special treats in their lunches with a resounding "Whoopie!" It's true—these delicious cream-filled treats will make you smile.

Many of you will already have all the equipment and tools that you need for the job of making whoopie pies: a large mixing bowl or two, measuring cups and measuring spoons, a good whisk, baking sheets.

techniques & equipment

If you are interested in getting a little more serious about your baking and want to achieve foolproof results, then I highly recommend a standing mixer such as a KitchenAid mixer. The flat beater paddle attachment will cream the butter and sugar until perfectly light and fluffy, and the whisk will give you billowy white meringues and Swiss buttercream icings.

A tool that I find indispensable in the Violet kitchen for making the whoopie pie cakes is the ice cream scoop. The ones with quick-release handles will give the perfect shape to your whoopies and they come in many different sizes. For most of the whoopie pie recipes here, I suggest a 1½-inch-diameter ice cream scoop with trigger for large whoopies and a small scoop for mini whoopies. They are available from good cookware stores and online. Or you can simply use a tablespoon or teaspoon to scoop up the mixture and a second one to scrape it onto your prepared baking sheets.

For filling whoopie pies, I use either a piping bag with a large round tip, or a couple of spoons. I scoop up the filling with one spoon and then scrape it off onto the flat side of one whoopie with the other. This works very well, but if you prefer a more perfect and refined whoopie, then use a piping bag and pipe perfect blobs onto half of your upturned whoopies and then sandwich them together, pressing until the filling comes to the edge.

For some of these recipes, you may need to bake the whoopie cakes in two batches, depending on the size of your oven and baking sheets. Unless otherwise specified, once the cakes come out of the oven transfer them to a wire rack, still on their baking sheets, and leave to cool before assembling the pies. Once assembled, most whoopie pies would keep overnight in an airtight container—if you can resist tempation that long.

I have recommended the particular fillings, toppings, and sauces that are ideal flavor combinations for each whoopie. But you can get creative and mix and match the recipes any way you like.

simple & sweet whoopie pies

. . . .

These are all the traditional whoopie pies you may have heard
of—plus a few more—that are perfect for a packed lunch or picnic
or an afternoon treat. A chocolate whoopie pie filled with
marshmallow cream is the quintessential whoopie pie, although
pumpkin and strawberry whoopie pies are now very popular. The
kitschy charm of red velvet cake translates well into a whoopie pie,
as does carrot cake. The lemon and mocha-orange whoopie pies
are filled with fresh cream and so may not travel as easily, but are
as light as air . . . and, well, rather addictive.

The whoopie pie that started it all: moist, spongy, dark chocolate cake sandwiched around a fluffy marshmallow center. Once you taste it, you'll understand what all the fuss is about.

chocolate whoopie pies

· ·

FILLING SUGGESTION: Fluffy Marshmallow (Recipe on page 4)
▶ Makes about 9 large or 24 mini whoopie pies

1¼ cups (175 g) all-purpose flour
¾ cup (100 g) unsweetened cocoa powder
1½ teaspoons baking soda
½ teaspoon baking powder
½ teaspoon salt
9 tablespoons (1 stick plus 1 tablespoon) unsalted butter, softened
1 cup (200 g) sugar
1 large egg
1 cup buttermilk
1 teaspoon pure vanilla extract

1. Preheat the oven to 350°F. Line two baking sheets with parchment paper.

2. In a bowl, sift together the flour, cocoa powder, baking soda, and baking powder. Stir in the salt and set aside.

3. In a separate bowl, cream the softened butter and sugar together until light and fluffy, using an electric hand mixer or a standing mixer fitted with the flat beater. Add the egg and mix well. Add the buttermilk and vanilla and beat until well combined. Slowly add the dry ingredients in two batches, mixing until just incorporated. Chill for 30 minutes before using.

4. Drop 18 large or 48 small scoops of batter, about 2 inches apart, onto the prepared baking sheets. Bake in the middle of the oven for 10–12 minutes for large whoopies or 8–10 minutes for mini whoopies, until the cakes are left with a slight impression when touched with a finger.

5. Remove from the oven to a wire rack and cool completely.

TO ASSEMBLE:
Spread or pipe a generous scoop of Fluffy Marshmallow Filling (page 4) onto the flat surface of a cooled whoopie. Top with another whoopie to make a sandwich, and serve.

fluffy marshmallow filling

▶ Makes enough to fill about 9 large or 24 mini whoopie pies

3 large egg whites
¾ cup (150 g) sugar
2 tablespoons golden syrup (see note)
Pinch of salt
1 teaspoon pure vanilla extract

1. Place all the ingredients into a heatproof bowl (the stainless-steel bowl of a standing mixer is ideal) and place the bowl over a saucepan of boiling water. Whisk continuously by hand until the sugar has dissolved and the mixture is frothy and slightly opaque (about 10–15 minutes).

2. Remove from the heat and whip the mixture on high speed in a standing mixer until it is white and thick and holds its shape.

3. Use immediately.

NOTE:
I highly recommend using golden syrup, even if it takes a bit of hunting to find some. However if you can't find golden syrup, you may substitute corn syrup—or for a closer match, Steen's pure cane syrup, which is available at www.steensyrup.com.

This variation combines the richness of cocoa and coffee with the sweet tanginess of candied orange peel for a truly grown-up whoopie pie.

mocha–orange whoopie pies

FILLING SUGGESTION: Espresso Cream (Recipe on page 9)
► Makes about 9 large or 24 mini whoopie pies

> 2 cups (280 g) all-purpose flour
> ½ cup (70 g) unsweetened cocoa powder
> 1 teaspoon baking soda
> ¼ teaspoon salt
> 7 tablespoons brewed strong coffee
> 7 tablespoons vegetable oil
> ½ cup whole milk
> 1 cup (200 g) sugar
> 1 large egg
> ¾ cup (175 g) chopped candied orange peel, plus extra for finishing

1. Preheat the oven to 350°F. Line two baking sheets with parchment paper.
2. In a bowl, sift together the flour, cocoa powder, and baking soda. Stir in the salt and set aside.
3. In a separate bowl, whisk together the coffee, oil, milk, and sugar. Whisk in the egg and stir in the candied peel. Slowly add the dry ingredients in two batches, mixing until just incorporated. Chill for 30 minutes.
4. Drop 18 large or 48 small scoops of batter, about 2 inches apart, onto the prepared baking sheets. Bake in the middle of the oven for 10–12 minutes for large whoopies or 8–10 minutes for mini whoopies, until the cakes are left with a slight impression when touched with a finger.
5. Remove from the oven to a wire rack and cool completely.

TO ASSEMBLE:
Spread a generous scoop of Espresso Cream (page 9) on the flat surface of a cooled whoopie. Top with another whoopie to make a sandwich. Once filled, chill for 10 minutes before rolling the sides of the whoopies in the extra candied peel.

espresso cream

· ·

▶ Makes enough to fill about 9 large or 24 mini whoopie pies

1½ cups heavy cream
2 tablespoons sugar
3 tablespoons strong brewed coffee, chilled
Scraped seeds of ½ vanilla pod
½ teaspoon pure vanilla extract
1 tablespoon finely ground espresso beans

1. Combine the heavy cream and sugar in a bowl and whip to very soft peaks, using an electric hand mixer or a standing mixer.

2. Add the coffee, vanilla seeds, and pure vanilla extract and whip again to soft peaks. Fold in the espresso beans and check the consistency. The cream should be thick enough to hold its shape without starting to turn to butter. (If it does get too thick, add a little unwhipped heavy cream.)

3. Chill in the fridge for 10 minutes before using. The cream will keep for a few days in a sealed container in the fridge, but may need to be rewhipped before using.

Pumpkin is one of our most popular whoopie pie flavors at my bakery, Violet. The spicy cake and its tangy cream cheese filling make the perfect pairing, especially in late autumn or early winter.

pumpkin whoopie pies

FILLING SUGGESTION: Cream Cheese (Recipe on page 12)
▶ Makes about 9 large or 24 mini whoopie pies

2 cups (280 g) all-purpose flour
½ teaspoon baking soda
1 teaspoon baking powder
1 teaspoon cinnamon
1 teaspoon ginger
¼ teaspoon cloves
¼ teaspoon mace
¼ teaspoon ground star anise (optional)
½ teaspoon salt
1 cup (200 g) dark brown sugar
½ cup vegetable oil
¾ cup (250 g) pumpkin purée, fresh or canned
¼ cup whole milk
1 large egg

1. Preheat the oven to 350°F. Line two baking sheets with parchment paper.
2. In a large bowl, whisk together the flour, baking soda, baking powder, spices, and salt, breaking up any clumps and making sure the leaveners and spices get well mixed in.
3. In a separate bowl, combine the brown sugar, vegetable oil, pumpkin purée, and milk until smooth. Add the egg and whisk to combine. Gradually add the dry ingredients, mixing well until fully incorporated. Chill for 30 minutes.
4. Drop 18 large or 48 small scoops of batter, about 2 inches apart, onto the prepared baking sheets. Bake in the middle of the oven for 10–12 minutes for large whoopies or 8–10 minutes for mini whoopies, until the cakes are left with a slight impression when touched with a finger.
5. Remove from the oven to a wire rack and cool completely.

TO ASSEMBLE:
Spread a generous scoop of Cream Cheese Filling (page 12) on the flat surface of a cooled whoopie. Top with another whoopie to make a sandwich, and serve.

cream cheese filling

· ·

▶ Makes enough to fill about 9 large or 24 mini whoopie pies

> 2⅔ cups (300 g) confectioners' sugar
> 4 tablespoons unsalted butter, softened
> 4 ounces cream cheese, softened
> ½ teaspoon pure vanilla extract
> 1 teaspoon maple syrup (optional)

1. Sift the confectioners' sugar in a bowl and set aside.

2. In a separate bowl, whip the softened butter until smooth, and creamy with no lumps, using an electric hand mixer or a standing mixer fitted with the flat beater. Add the cream cheese and whip together, scraping down the bowl once. Gradually add the sifted confectioners' sugar until the mixture comes together in a light and fluffy texture. Add the vanilla and the maple syrup (if using) and mix well.

3. Use right away or chill until ready to use. Will keep in a sealed container in the fridge for up to 7 days.

I'm not usually a fan of cooked strawberries, but this is one of my favorite whoopie pies. A cross between strawberry shortcake and a muffin, it's a great one for the strawberry season.

strawberry whoopie pies

FILLING SUGGESTION: Strawberry Buttercream (Recipe on page 16)
▶ Makes about 9 large or 24 mini whoopie pies

¾ cup fresh ripe strawberries
2 cups plus 2 tablespoons (300 g) all-purpose flour
1½ teaspoons baking soda
½ teaspoon baking powder
¼ teaspoon salt
1 cup (200 g) light brown sugar
⅓ cup vegetable oil
¼ cup buttermilk
1 large egg
Confectioners' sugar for dusting

1. Preheat the oven to 350°F. Line two baking sheets with parchment paper.
2. Put the strawberries in a food processor and pulse until they are chopped but not puréed. Set aside. In a bowl, sift together the flour, baking soda, and baking powder. Stir in the salt and set aside.
3. Combine the brown sugar and oil in a large bowl and mix well with a wooden spoon. Stir in the chopped strawberries and the buttermilk until just combined, then whisk in the egg. Fold in the flour mixture in two batches, taking care not to overmix the batter. Chill for 30 minutes.
4. Drop 18 large or 48 small scoops of batter, about 2 inches apart, onto the prepared baking sheets. Bake in the middle of the oven for 10–12 minutes for large whoopies or 8–10 minutes for mini whoopies, until the cakes are left with a slight impression when touched with a finger.
5. Remove from the oven to a wire rack and cool completely.

TO ASSEMBLE:
Spread a generous scoop of Strawberry Buttercream (page 16) on the flat surface of a cooled whoopie. Top with another whoopie to make a sandwich, dust with confectioners' sugar, and serve.

strawberry buttercream

▶ Makes enough to fill about 9 large or 24 mini whoopie pies

About ½ cup unhulled berries
6 tablespoons very soft unsalted butter
4 to 6 cups (500–750 g) confectioners' sugar, sifted
½ teaspoon pure vanilla extract
½ teaspoon fresh lemon juice

1. Rinse and hull the strawberries, then purée them in a food processor (you should have ¼ cup purée).

2. In a bowl, cream together the butter and 4 cups confectioners' sugar with an electric hand mixer or on a low speed in a standing mixer fitted with the flat beater. Gradually add the vanilla, lemon juice, and strawberry purée. Gradually mix in another 5 cups confectioners' sugar on a low speed for about 3 minutes, until the mixture has a light and fluffy texture and the sugar has dissolved. Add more sugar if the mixture seems too soft (the amount needed varies according to the air temperature and acidity of the fruit).

3. Use right away or store in a sealed container in the fridge for up to 7 days. Bring it to room temperature before using and beat on a low speed to make it creamy again.

When these are freshly baked and the weather is warm, the melt-in-your-mouth softness of the chocolate chips is simply sensational.

chocolate chip whoopie pies

FILLING SUGGESTION: Chocolate Marshmallow (Recipe on page 20)
▶ Makes about 9 large or 24 mini whoopie pies

> 2 cups (280 g) all-purpose flour
> 1 teaspoon baking powder
> 1½ teaspoons baking soda
> ¼ teaspoon salt
> 9 tablespoons (1 stick plus 1 tablespoon) unsalted butter, softened
> ½ cup (100 g) sugar
> ½ cup (100 g) light brown sugar
> 1 large egg
> ½ cup buttermilk
> 1 teaspoon pure vanilla extract
> 1¼ cups dark chocolate chips

1. Preheat the oven to 350°F. Line two baking sheets with parchment paper.

2. In a bowl, sift together the flour, baking powder, and baking soda. Stir in the salt and set aside.

3. In a separate bowl, cream the softened butter, and sugars together until light and fluffy, using an electric hand mixer or a standing mixer fitted with the flat beater. Add the egg and mix well. Measure the buttermilk into a liquid measuring cup and add the vanilla. Pour this into the butter mixture and beat until well combined. Slowly add the dry ingredients in two batches, mixing until just incorporated. Stir in the chocolate chips. Chill for 30 minutes.

4. Drop 18 large or 48 small scoops of batter, about 2 inches apart, onto the prepared baking sheets. Bake in the middle of the oven for 10–12 minutes for large whoopies or 8–10 minutes for mini whoopies, until the cakes are left with a slight impression when touched with a finger.

5. Remove from the oven to a wire rack and cool completely.

TO ASSEMBLE:
Pipe or spread a generous scoop of Chocolate Marshmallow Filling (page 20) on the flat surface of a cooled whoopie. Top with another whoopie to make a sandwich, and serve.

chocolate marshmallow filling

▶ Makes enough to fill about 9 large or 24 mini whoopie pies

4 ounces dark chocolate, broken into small pieces
3 large egg whites
¾ cup (150 g) sugar
2 tablespoons golden syrup
Pinch of salt
1 teaspoon pure vanilla extract

1. Melt the chocolate in a heatproof bowl over a pan of barely simmering water. Once the chocolate has melted, take the bowl off the pan and let it cool slightly while you prepare the marshmallow.

2. Place the saucepan of water back on the heat and bring to a boil. Place the remaining ingredients into the stainless-steel bowl of a standing mixer and then place the bowl over the pan. Whisk continuously by hand until the sugar has dissolved and the mixture is frothy and slightly opaque (about 10–15 minutes).

3. Remove the bowl from the heat and transfer to the mixer. Whip the mixture on high speed until it is white and thick and holds its shape. Fold in the melted chocolate.

4. Use immediately.

We tend to think of carrot cake as a healthier option than other cakes simply because it has a vegetable in it, and we generally feel less guilty about eating it, too. The same goes for this carrot cake whoopie pie.

carrot cake whoopie pies

FILLING SUGGESTION: Orange Mascarpone Cream (Recipe on page 24)
▶ Makes about 9 large or 24 small whoopie pies

1¾ cups (250 g) all-purpose flour
1 teaspoon baking soda
½ teaspoon baking powder
½ teaspoon cinnamon
½ teaspoon ground ginger
¼ teaspoon salt
9 tablespoons (1 stick plus 1 tablespoon) unsalted butter, softened
½ cup (100 g) sugar
½ cup (100 g) light brown sugar
1 large egg
1 teaspoon pure vanilla extract
2 carrots, peeled and grated
Zest of 1 orange

1. Preheat the oven to 350°F. Line two baking sheets with parchment paper.
2. In a bowl, sift together flour, baking soda, baking powder, cinnamon, and ginger. Stir in the salt and set aside.
3. In a separate bowl, cream the softened butter, and sugars until light and fluffy, using an electric hand mixer or a standing mixer fitted with the flat beater. Add the egg and vanilla and mix well. Add the grated carrot and orange zest and mix well. Finally, add the dry ingredients, mixing until just incorporated. Chill for 30 minutes.
4. Drop 18 large or 48 small scoops of batter, about 2 inches apart, onto the prepared baking sheets. Bake in the middle of the oven for 10–12 minutes for large whoopies and 8–10 minutes for mini whoopies, until the cakes are left with a slight impression when touched with a finger.
5. Remove from the oven to a wire rack and cool completely.

TO ASSEMBLE:
Spread a generous scoop of Orange Mascarpone Cream (page 24) on the flat surface of a cooled whoopie. Top with another whoopie to make a sandwich, and serve.

orange mascarpone cream

· ·

▶ Makes enough to fill about 9 large or 24 mini whoopie pies

> **8 ounces cream cheese**
> **⅔ cup mascarpone cheese**
> **1 cup (100 g) confectioners' sugar**
> **Zest and juice of ½ orange**

1. Place the cream cheese in a bowl and whisk until smooth. Add the mascarpone cheese and whisk again.

2. Sift the confectioners' sugar into the bowl to make sure there are no lumps, and mix until smooth. Add the orange zest and juice and mix to combine.

3. Use immediately, or store in a sealed container in the fridge for up to 3 days.

Lemon imparts a lovely fresh flavor to cakes and puddings. It's worth seeking out good-quality lemons. Meyer lemons are exceptional and more readily available than ever.

lemon cream whoopie pies

. . . .

FILLING SUGGESTION: Lemon Curd Cream (Recipe on page 28)
▶ Makes about 9 large or 24 mini whoopie pies

> 2 cups plus 2 tablespoons (300 g) all-purpose flour
> 1 teaspoon baking powder
> ¼ teaspoon baking soda
> ¼ teaspoon salt
> 9 tablespoons (1 stick plus 1 tablespoon) unsalted butter, softened
> 1 cup (200 g) sugar
> 1 large egg
> 1 teaspoon pure vanilla extract
> 6 tablespoons whole milk
> 3 tablespoons fresh lemon juice
> Zest of 2 medium lemons

1. Preheat the oven to 350°F. Line two baking sheets with parchment paper.
2. In a bowl, sift together the flour, baking powder, and baking soda. Stir in the salt and set aside.
3. In a separate bowl, cream the softened butter and the sugar together until light and fluffy, using an electric hand mixer or a standing mixer fitted with the flat beater. Add the egg and mix well. In a liquid measuring cup, combine the vanilla, milk, and lemon juice. Add this to the butter mixture and mix well. Add the dry ingredients, mixing until just incorporated. Finally, fold in the lemon zest. Chill for 30 minutes.
4. Drop 18 large or 48 small scoops of batter, about 2 inches apart, onto the prepared baking sheets. Bake in the middle of the oven for 10–12 minutes for large whoopies or 8–10 minutes for mini whoopies, until the cakes are left with a slight impression when touched with a finger.
5. Remove from the oven to a wire rack and cool completely.

TO ASSEMBLE:
Spread a generous scoop of Lemon Curd Cream (page 28) on the flat surface of a cooled whoopie. Top with another whoopie to make a sandwich, and serve.

lemon curd cream

> Makes enough to fill about 9 large or 24 mini whoopie pies

½ cup (100 g) sugar
Pinch of salt
Zest and juice of 2 medium lemons
2 large egg yolks
3 sticks (1½ cups) cold unsalted butter, cut into cubes
3 tablespoons heavy cream

1. Put the sugar, salt, lemon zest and juice, and egg yolks in a medium-sized, heatproof bowl. Place the bowl over a saucepan of barely simmering water and warm gently, whisking constantly. Add the butter, a few cubes at a time, stirring constantly until all the butter is incorporated and the mixture is smooth and thick. Do not overheat or the eggs will scramble. Strain to remove the zest and any eggy bits. Cover with plastic wrap, pressing it down on the surface of the custard. Leave to cool for 20 minutes, then chill for 2 hours before using.

2. The lemon curd will keep in a sealed container in the fridge for up to 3 days. When ready to use, whip the heavy cream and fold into the chilled custard.

Every summer my grandmother made me a "Red Cake" topped with a fluffy white frosting made with a flour roux. This will forever remind me of her.

red velvet whoopie pies

· ·

FILLING SUGGESTION: Old-fashioned Buttercream (Recipe on page 32)
▶ Makes about 9 large or 24 mini whoopie pies

2 cups (280 g) all-purpose flour
6 tablespoons cornstarch
¼ teaspoon salt
7 tablespoons unsalted butter, softened
1 cup (200 g) sugar
1 large egg
¼ cup unsweetened cocoa powder
3 tablespoons red food coloring
1½ teaspoons pure vanilla extract
¾ cup buttermilk
1½ teaspoons baking soda
1½ teaspoons white vinegar

1. Preheat the oven to 350°F. Line two baking sheets with parchment paper.
2. Sift the flours together and stir in the salt. Set aside.
3. In the bowl of a standing mixer fitted with the flat beater, cream the butter and the sugar together until light and fluffy. Add the egg and mix well. In another bowl, use a fork to combine the cocoa powder, food coloring, and vanilla into a thick paste. Add to the creamed butter and mix well. Add half the buttermilk and mix well. Add half the sifted flour, beating until just mixed. Add the remaining buttermilk, mixing until well combined, then add the remaining flour.
4. In a small bowl, dissolve the baking soda in the vinegar and add to the cake mixture, scraping it out with a rubber spatula. Beat for a couple of minutes but no longer.
5. Drop 18 large or 48 small scoops of batter, about 2 inches apart, onto the prepared baking sheets. Bake in the middle of the oven for 10–12 minutes for large whoopies or 8–10 minutes for mini whoopies.
6. Remove from the oven to a wire rack and cool completely.

TO ASSEMBLE:
Spread a generous scoop of Old-fashioned Buttercream (page 32) on a cooled cake. Top with another cake to make a sandwich, and serve.

old-fashioned buttercream

· ·

½ cup whole milk
2 tablespoons all-purpose flour
½ cup (100 g) sugar
¼ teaspoon salt
4 tablespoons unsalted butter, softened
4 tablespoons vegetable shortening
1 teaspoon pure vanilla extract

1. Whisk together the milk and flour in a small saucepan, using an electric hand mixer. Place over a moderate heat until the mixture just begins to thicken. Set aside to cool.

2. In a bowl, beat together the sugar, salt, butter, and shortening until light and fluffy, using an electric hand mixer or a standing mixer. Add the vanilla and beat well. Add the flour mixture and beat for 3 minutes.

3. Chill until ready to use. It will keep in a sealed container in the fridge for up to 5 days. Bring to room temperature and beat again with a flat beater before using.

Violet's salted caramel cupcake is a particular favorite of our male customers, so we often call it "the man's cupcake." Here's a whoopie pie for the boys.

salty caramel whoopie pies

FILLING SUGGESTION: Caramel Swiss Buttercream (Recipe on page 38)
▶ Makes about 9 large or 24 mini whoopie pies

> 2 cups plus 2 tablespoons (300 g) all-purpose flour
> 2 teaspoons baking powder
> ½ teaspoon salt
> 9 tablespoons (1 stick plus 1 tablespoon) unsalted butter, softened
> ½ cup whole milk
> 1 cup (200 g) light brown sugar
> 2 large eggs
> 1 teaspoon pure vanilla extract

1. Preheat the oven to 350°F. Line two baking sheets with parchment paper.
2. In a bowl, sift together the flour and baking powder. Stir in the salt and set aside. In a small saucepan, melt the butter with the milk, but don't let it boil. Remove from the heat and pour into a small bowl to cool.
3. In a separate bowl, beat together the brown sugar, eggs, and vanilla until light and fluffy, using an electric hand mixer or a standing mixer. Add the dry ingredients, mixing until just incorporated. Pour in the cooled milk mixture and stir until just combined. Chill for 30 minutes.
4. Drop 18 large or 48 small scoops of batter, about 2 inches apart, onto the prepared baking sheets. Bake in the middle of the oven for 10–12 minutes for large whoopies or 8–10 minutes for mini whoopies, until the cakes are left with a slight impression when touched with a finger.
5. Remove from the oven to a wire rack and cool completely.

TO ASSEMBLE:
Spread a generous scoop of Caramel Swiss Buttercream (page 38) on the flat surface of a cooled whoopie. Top with another whoopie to make a sandwich, and serve.

caramel swiss buttercream

· ·

▶ Makes enough to fill about 9 large or 24 mini whoopie pies

> 3 tablespoons heavy cream
> ½ cup (75 g) sugar, plus 2 tablespoons (50 g)
> 2 tablespoons water
> 12 tablespoons (1½ sticks) unsalted butter, softened
> ¼ teaspoon salt
> 2 large egg whites
> ½ teaspoon pure vanilla extract

1. Have a whisk and the cream ready to use near the stove.

2. Combine the ½ cup sugar and the water in a heavy-bottomed saucepan over medium heat. Swirl the pan occasionally to help dissolve the sugar, but do not stir. Turn the heat up to high and bring the syrup to a boil. Cook, without stirring, until it becomes very dark caramel in color. Turn off the heat and pour in the cream, whisking continuously (be careful as it will spatter). Transfer to a heatproof container to cool completely.

3. In a bowl, beat the butter and salt with an electric hand mixer until fluffy.

4. In the stainless-steel bowl of a standing mixer, combine the 2 tablespoons sugar with the egg whites. Place over a saucepan of barely simmering water and whisk continuously by hand until the sugar has dissolved and the mixture is frothy and slightly opaque (about 10–15 minutes).

5. Transfer the bowl of egg whites to the standing mixer and whisk until fluffy and cooled (about another 10 minutes). Once the mixture is cool enough, start adding the creamed butter. The mixture will curdle but then come back together. Switch to the flat beater and, mixing on medium speed, pour in the caramel.

6. If not using right away, store in a sealed container in the fridge for up to 5 days. Bring to room temperature and beat with a flat beater before using again.

iced & glazed whoopie pies

. . . .

Whoopie pies are, by design, quite plain looking—a simple
sandwiching of cake and filling. Adding a thin glaze dotted with
crushed rose petals or piped melted chocolate transforms them
into something really beautiful. I've also slipped in a meringue
here and although, technically, it's not a whoopie pie, its size and
shape are so similar that I thought it made a nice addition to this
chapter. These whoopie pies, served in individual paper cases and
stacked in towers on cake stands, would be great for a wedding or
celebration.

Inspired by the British classic Tunnock's Teacake, this whoopie pie combines soft, rich vanilla cake, fluffy marshmallow filling, and chocolate glaze to create an indulgent, retro-style pie.

teacake whoopie pies

· ·

FILLING SUGGESTION: Fluffy Marshmallow (Recipe on page 4)
GLAZE SUGGESTION: Chocolate Glaze (Recipe on page 44)
▶ Makes about 9 large or 24 mini whoopie pies

> 2 cups (280 g) all-purpose flour
> ¼ teaspoon baking powder
> ¼ teaspoon baking soda
> Pinch of salt
> 10½ tablespoons (1 stick plus 2½ tablespoons) unsalted butter, softened
> ½ cup plus 2 tablespoons (125 g) sugar
> 3 large egg yolks
> 3 tablespoons heavy cream
> 1 teaspoon pure vanilla extract

1. Preheat the oven to 350°F. Line two baking sheets with parchment paper.
2. In a bowl, sift together the flour, baking powder, and baking soda. Stir in the salt and set aside.
3. In the bowl of a standing mixer fitted with the flat beater, cream the softened butter and the sugar until light and fluffy. Add the egg yolks, one at a time, and mix well. Measure the cream into a liquid measuring cup and stir in the vanilla. Pour the liquid into the butter mixture and beat until well combined. Add the dry ingredients in one batch, mixing until just incorporated. Chill for 30 minutes.
4. Drop 18 large or 48 small scoops of batter, about 2 inches apart, onto the prepared baking sheets. Bake in the middle of the oven for 10–12 minutes for large whoopies or 8–10 minutes for mini whoopies, until the cakes are left with a slight impression when touched with a finger.
5. Remove from the oven to a wire rack and cool completely.

TO ASSEMBLE:
Spread or pipe a generous scoop of Fluffy Marshmallow Filling (page 4) on the flat surface of a cooled whoopie. Top with another whoopie, then spoon or pipe a generous amount of Chocolate Glaze (page 44) on top. Let the chocolate set completely before serving (up to 1 hour).

chocolate glaze

· ·

▶ Makes enough to cover about 9 large or 24 mini whoopie pies

1¼ pounds milk or dark chocolate, such as Valrhona

1. Finely chop the chocolate. Place half of the chopped chocolate in a heatproof bowl that will fit snugly over one of your saucepans.

2. Pour water into the saucepan to come about ¾ inch up the sides, and heat to barely simmering. Place the bowl of chocolate over the pan to melt the chocolate, making sure the bottom of the bowl does not come into contact with the water. Now turn the heat off, but do not remove the bowl from the pan, as this would release the steam that is needed to melt the chocolate. Stir the chocolate occasionally to aid the melting. Once it's melted, add the remaining chopped chocolate and then remove the bowl from the saucepan. Place the chocolate in a warm part of the kitchen, away from any drafts, to finish melting. Wait until the chocolate has melted fully (this will take about 10 minutes) before spooning or piping over the whoopie pies.

The exotic flavors of delicate rosewater, tender pistachios, and sweet cherry liqueur might seem strange in a whoopie pie, but the evocation of the taste and texture of soft nougat is lovely here.

rose-pistachio whoopie pies

FILLING SUGGESTION: Kirsch Swiss Buttercream (Recipe on page 48)
GLAZE SUGGESTION: Rosewater Icing (Recipe on page 50)
▶ Makes about 9 large or 24 mini whoopie pies

2 cups plus 2 tablespoons (300 g) all-purpose flour
1 teaspoon baking soda
½ teaspoon salt
9 tablespoons (1 stick plus 1 tablespoon) unsalted butter, softened
1 cup (200 g) sugar
1 large egg
½ teaspoon rosewater
¾ cup buttermilk
¾ cup pistachios, finely chopped or ground, plus extra for sprinkling
1 cup ground almonds
Crushed candied rose petals, for garnishing

1. Preheat the oven to 350°F. Line two baking sheets with parchment paper.
2. In a bowl, sift together the flour and baking soda. Stir in the salt and set aside. In a separate bowl, cream together the butter and sugar until light and fluffy, using an electric hand mixer or a standing mixer fitted with the flat beater. Add the egg and mix well. Measure the rosewater and buttermilk into a liquid measuring cup and then add half of this to the butter mixture. Slowly add the dry ingredients, mixing until just incorporated. Add the remaining buttermilk mixture until well combined and then fold in the ground nuts. Chill for 30 minutes.
3. Drop 18 large or 48 small scoops of batter, about 2 inches apart, onto the prepared baking sheets. Bake in the middle of the oven for 10–12 minutes for large whoopies or 8–10 minutes for mini whoopies, until the cakes are left with a slight impression when touched with a finger.
4. Remove from the oven to a wire rack and cool completely.

TO ASSEMBLE:
Pipe or spread a generous scoop of Kirsch Swiss Buttercream (page 48) on the flat surface of a cooled whoopie. Top with another whoopie and drizzle with Rosewater Icing (page 50). Sprinkle with the remaining chopped pistachios and some crushed candied rose petals.

kirsch swiss buttercream

▶ Makes enough to fill about 9 large or 24 mini whoopie pies

2 sticks (1 cup) unsalted butter, softened
3 large egg whites
½ cup (100 g) sugar
1 tablespoon golden syrup
1 tablespoon Kirsch cherry liqueur

1. In a bowl, beat the butter until fluffy, using an electric hand mixer or a standing mixer fitted with the flat beater, and set aside. In the bowl of a standing mixer, combine the three large egg whites with the sugar and golden syrup. Place over a saucepan of barely simmering water and whisk continuously by hand until the sugar has dissolved and the mixture is frothy and slightly opaque (10–15 minutes).

2. Transfer the bowl of egg whites to the standing mixer, add the Kirsch, and whisk until fluffy and cooled (about 10 minutes). Once cool, start adding the creamed butter in batches, whisking well after each addition. The mixture will curdle but then come back together again. Switch to the flat beater and beat for 3 minutes more.

3. Will keep in a sealed container in the fridge for up to 5 days. Bring to room temperature and beat with a flat beater before using.

rosewater icing

. . . .

▶ Makes enough to cover about 9 large or 24 mini whoopie pies

1¾ cups (200 g) confectioners' sugar
2 teaspoons rosewater

Sift the confectioners' sugar into a small bowl and then whisk in the rosewater until smooth. If you prefer a thicker consistency spread on top of the whoopie pie, add slightly more confectioners' sugar to adjust.

plain icing

. . . .

Substitute 2 teaspoons water for the rosewater.

The Walnut Whip, another nostalgic British treat, is actually a fantastic combination of flavors. This whoopie pie honors those flavors while improving on the quality of ingredients.

walnut whip whoopie pies

FILLING SUGGESTION: Vanilla Swiss Buttercream (Recipe on page 54)
GLAZE SUGGESTION: Chocolate Glaze (Recipe on page 44)
▶ Makes about 9 large or 24 mini whoopie pies

>   2 cups plus 2 tablespoons (300 g) all-purpose flour
>   1 teaspoon baking soda
>   ½ teaspoon salt
>   9 tablespoons (1 stick plus 1 tablespoon) unsalted butter, softened
>   1 cup (200 g) sugar
>   1 large egg
>   1 teaspoon pure vanilla extract
>   ¾ cup buttermilk
>   1 cup walnuts, finely chopped or ground, plus extra for garnishing
>   1 cup ground almonds

1. Preheat the oven to 350°F. Line two baking sheets with parchment paper.
2. In a bowl, sift together the flour and baking soda. Stir in the salt and set aside.
3. In a separate bowl, cream together the butter and sugar until light and fluffy, using an electric hand mixer or a standing mixer fitted with the flat beater. Add the egg and mix well. Measure the vanilla and buttermilk into a liquid measuring cup and add half of this to the butter mixture. Slowly add the dry ingredients, mixing until just incorporated. Add the remaining buttermilk until well combined, then fold in the ground nuts. Chill for 30 minutes.
4. Drop 18 large or 48 small scoops of batter, about 2 inches apart, onto the prepared baking sheets. Bake in the middle of the oven for 10–12 minutes for large whoopies or 8–10 minutes for mini whoopies, until the cakes are left with a slight impression when touched with a finger.
5. Remove from the oven to a wire rack and cool completely.

TO ASSEMBLE:
Pipe or spread a generous scoop of Vanilla Swiss Buttercream (page 54) on the flat surface of a cooled whoopie. Top with another whoopie, then add a generous piping of Chocolate Glaze (page 44) and garnish with chopped walnuts. Let the chocolate set before serving (up to 1 hour).

vanilla swiss buttercream

▶ Makes enough to fill about 9 large or 24 mini whoopie pies

2 sticks (1 cup) unsalted butter, softened
3 large egg whites
½ cup (100 g) sugar
1 tablespoon golden syrup
Scraped seeds of ½ vanilla pod
1 teaspoon pure vanilla extract

1. In a bowl, beat the butter until fluffy, using an electric hand mixer or a standing mixer. In the bowl of a standing mixer, combine the egg whites with the sugar, golden syrup, and the vanilla seeds. Place the bowl over a saucepan of barely simmering water and whisk continuously by hand until the sugar has dissolved and the mixture is frothy and slightly opaque (about 10–15 minutes).

2. Transfer the bowl of egg whites to the standing mixer, add the vanilla, and whisk until fluffy and cooled (about 10 minutes). Once cool, start adding the creamed butter in batches, whisking well after each addition. The mixture will curdle but then come back together again. Switch to the flat beater and beat for 3 minutes more.

3. Will keep in a sealed container in the fridge for up to 5 days. Bring to room temperature and beat with a flat beater before using.

A hot chocolate and an individual Mont Blanc with my mom at Café Angelina in Paris were the inspiration for this whoopie pie. Use a good-quality chestnut spread in the filling or make your own.

meringue whoopie pies

· ·

FILLING SUGGESTION: Chestnut Cream (Recipe on page 60)
ICING SUGGESTION: Vanilla Bean Cream (Recipe on page 72)
▶ Makes about 9 large or 24 mini whoopie pies

> 3 large egg whites
> ¼ teaspoon salt
> ½ teaspoon white vinegar
> 1 teaspoon pure vanilla extract
> 1 cup (200 g) sugar
> 1½ teaspoons cornstarch

1. Preheat the oven to 225°F. Line two baking sheets with parchment paper.
2. In the bowl of a standing mixer, beat together the egg whites, salt, vinegar, and vanilla on a high speed until soft peaks form.
3. In a separate bowl, whisk the sugar and cornstarch together by hand and then add half this mixture to the frothy egg whites. Whisk until very stiff, then add the remaining sugar and cornstarch mixture and whisk until smooth and glossy.
4. Drop 9 large or 24 small scoops of meringue, about 1½ inches apart, onto the prepared baking sheets. Bake in the middle of the oven for about 2½ hours for large whoopies or 1 hour for mini whoopies, until the meringues are baked firm on the outside.
5. Remove from the oven and immediately transfer the meringues off the baking sheet and onto a wire rack, peeling off the parchment paper, and leave to cool completely before filling.

TO ASSEMBLE:
Simply break open or use a serrated knife to split each meringue. Spread a generous scoop of Chestnut Cream (page 60) on the bottom half. Top with the other meringue half and then spoon a generous amount of Vanilla Bean Cream (page 72) over the top.

chestnut cream

· ·

▶ Makes enough to fill about 9 large or 24 mini whoopie pies

6½ tablespoons unsalted butter, softened
1 cup (100 g) confectioners' sugar
1 cup chestnut purée (crème de marrons)
Pinch of salt

1. Beat together the softened butter and confectioners' sugar until smooth, using an electric hand mixer or a standing mixer fitted with the flat beater. Add the chestnut spread and salt and beat until smooth.

2. The filling can be made ahead and will keep for up to a week in a sealed container in the fridge.

White and frosty, this whoopie pie uses coconut milk and a hit of rum to give it a seriously tropical flavor. I've discovered that coconut isn't to everyone's taste, but I find the perfume intoxicating.

coconut cream whoopie pies

FILLING SUGGESTION: Coconut Swiss Buttercream (Recipe on page 64)
ICING SUGGESTION: Coconut Glaze (Recipe on page 66)
▶ Makes about 9 large or 24 mini whoopie pies

1¾ cups (250 g) all-purpose flour
2 teaspoons baking powder
½ teaspoon baking soda
¼ teaspoon salt
9 tablespoons (1 stick plus 1 tablespoon) unsalted butter, softened
1 cup (200 g) sugar
2 large eggs
1 teaspoon pure vanilla extract
1 tablespoon white rum
½ cup coconut milk
½ cup shredded coconut, plus extra for sprinkling

1. Preheat the oven to 350°F. Line two baking sheets with parchment paper.
2. In a bowl, sift together the flour and baking powder and baking soda. Stir in the salt and set aside.
3. In a separate bowl, cream the butter and sugar until light and fluffy with an electric hand mixer or in a standing mixer fitted with the flat beater. Add the eggs, one at a time, and mix well. In a liquid measuring cup, combine the vanilla, rum, and coconut milk. Add this to the butter mixture and mix well. Add the dry ingredients, mixing until just incorporated. Finally, fold in the shredded coconut. Chill for 30 minutes.
4. Drop 18 large or 48 small scoops of batter, about 2 inches apart, onto the prepared baking sheets. Bake in the middle of the oven for 10–12 minutes for large whoopies or 8–10 minutes for mini whoopies, until the cakes are left with a slight impression when touched with a finger.
5. Remove from the oven to a wire rack and cool completely.

TO ASSEMBLE:
Spread a generous scoop of Coconut Swiss Buttercream (page 64) on the flat surface of a cooled cake. Top with another cake, then spread with Coconut Glaze (page 66) and sprinkle with more coconut.

coconut swiss buttercream

▶ Makes enough to fill about 9 large or 24 mini whoopie pies

2 large egg whites
½ cup (100 g) sugar
¼ teaspoon salt
1 tablespoon golden syrup
12 tablespoons (1½ sticks) unsalted butter, softened
4½ teapoons coconut milk
1 teaspoon pure vanilla extract
1 teaspoon white rum

1. Combine the egg whites, sugar, and salt in the bowl of a standing mixer. Place over a saucepan of barely simmering water and whisk continuously by hand until the sugar has dissolved and the mixture is frothy and slightly opaque (10–15 minutes). Transfer to the mixer and whisk until fluffy peaks form and the mixture has cooled (about 10 minutes).

2. Turn the mixer down to a low speed and add the butter in batches. Mix well after each addition and scrape down the bowl from time to time. The mixture will curdle but then come back together again. Switch to the flat beater and beat for a few minutes more. In a liquid measuring cup, whisk together the coconut milk, vanilla, and rum. Pour this into the mixture and beat until smooth.

3. Will keep in a sealed container in the fridge for up to 5 days. Bring to room temperature and beat with a flat beater before using.

the whoopie pie book

coconut glaze

· ·

▶ Makes enough to cover about 9 large or 24 mini whoopie pies

1¾ cups (200 g) confectioners' sugar
2 tablespoons coconut milk

Sift the confectioners' sugar into a small bowl and then whisk in the coconut milk until smooth. If you prefer a thicker consistency spread on top of the whoopie, add slightly more confectioners' sugar to adjust.

topped & drizzled whoopie pies

· ·

The larger-sized whoopie pie can sometimes be a bit intimidating
for one person as a snack. At Violet we often serve them on a plate
with two forks, for a couple or friends to share. This inspired me to
create whoopie pies that would make delicious desserts or dinner
finales, with billowy cream fillings and drizzled with syrupy sauces.
The blackberry whoopie pies, which use fresh, ripe blackberries
embellished with rose geranium from the Violet garden, are a
particular favorite, while the banana cream whoopie pies are totally
decadent.

Flecked with fresh fruit, this stylish whoopie pie, with its elegant assembly, is a great party dessert for the summer months. Always choose the best fruit available.

raspberry & nectarine whoopie pies

FILLING SUGGESTION: Vanilla Bean Cream (Recipe on page 72)
DRIZZLE SUGGESTION: Raspberry Sauce (Recipe on page 74)
▶ Makes about 9 large or 24 mini whoopie pies

1¾ cups (250 g) all-purpose flour
½ teaspoon baking powder
1½ teaspoons baking soda
¼ teaspoon salt
9 tablespoons (1 stick plus 1 tablespoon) unsalted butter, softened
1 cup (200 g) sugar
1 large egg
1 teaspoon pure vanilla extract
3 tablespoons whole milk
1 teaspoon fresh lemon juice
2 small ripe nectarines, pitted and chopped into ¼-inch dice, plus 3 more, sliced for
   serving
1 cup fresh raspberries, halved

1. Preheat the oven to 350°F. Line two baking sheets with parchment paper.
2. In a bowl, sift together the flour, baking powder, and baking soda. Stir in the salt and set aside. In a separate bowl, cream the butter and sugar together until light and fluffy, using an electric hand mixer or a standing mixer fitted with the flat beater. Add the egg and vanilla and mix well. Measure the milk into a liquid measuring cup and add the lemon juice (the juice will curdle the milk, which is what you want), then beat this into the butter mixture. Gently stir in the prepared fruit. Slowly add the dry ingredients, mixing until just incorporated. Chill for 30 minutes.
3. Drop 18 large or 48 small scoops of batter, about 2 inches apart, onto the prepared baking sheets. Bake in the middle of the oven for 10–12 minutes for large whoopies or 8–10 minutes for mini whoopies, until the cakes are left with a slight impression when touched with a finger.
4. Remove from the oven to a wire rack and cool completely.

TO ASSEMBLE:
Spread a generous scoop of Vanilla Bean Cream (page 72) on a cooled cake. Add the wedges of nectarines and drizzle with Raspberry Sauce (page 74). Top with another cake and drizzle with more sauce.

vanilla bean cream

· ·

▶ Makes enough to fill about 9 large or 24 mini whoopie pies

> 1¾ cups heavy cream
> 2 tablespoons sugar
> Scraped seeds of ½ vanilla pod
> 1 teaspoon pure vanilla extract

1. Put all the ingredients into a large bowl and whisk until the mixture begins to thicken. Taste for sugar and adjust as needed, bearing in mind what other ingredients you will be using to assemble the whoopie pies and how sweet or "unsweet" they are.

2. Chill until needed. Will keep for 3 days in a sealed container in the fridge but may require more whipping before using.

raspberry sauce

· ·

▶ Makes enough to drizzle over 9 large or 24 mini whoopie pies

3 cups fresh raspberries
2 tablespoons confectioners' sugar
1 teaspoon Kirsch cherry liqueur (optional)

1. Purée the raspberries and sugar in a food processor or blender, or crush the berries with the back of a wooden spoon, then add the sugar and mix well. Strain the puréed raspberries through a fine mesh sieve and discard the seeds. Stir in the Kirsch (if using). Taste and add more sugar if needed.

2. Chill until ready to use. Will keep in a sealed container in the fridge for 2 days.

Rose geranium has a delicate flavor that goes well with berries, as in the sauce below, but you may have to grow your own. The leaves are especially fragrant in summer when blackberries are at their peak.

blackberry whoopie pies

FILLING SUGGESTION: Blackberry Cream (Recipe on page 78)
DRIZZLE SUGGESTION: Blackberry-Geranium Sauce (Recipe on page 80)
▶ Makes about 9 large or 24 mini whoopie pies

    1¾ cups (250 g) all-purpose flour
    ½ teaspoon baking powder
    1½ teaspoons baking soda
    ¼ teaspoon salt
    9 tablespoons (1 stick plus 1 tablespoon) unsalted butter, softened
    1 cup (200 g) sugar
    1 large egg
    1 teaspoon pure vanilla extract
    3 tablespoons whole milk
    1 teaspoon fresh lemon juice
    1¼ cups fresh blackberries

1. Preheat the oven to 350°F. Line two baking sheets with parchment paper.
2. In a bowl, sift together the flour, baking powder, and baking soda. Stir in the salt and set aside. In a separate bowl, cream the butter and sugar together until light and fluffy, using an electric hand mixer or a standing mixer fitted with the flat beater. Add the egg and vanilla and mix well. Measure the milk into a liquid measuring cup and add the lemon juice (this will curdle the milk, which is what you want) and beat this into the butter mixture. Add the dry ingredients, mixing until just incorporated. Chill for 30 minutes.
3. Drop 18 large or 48 small scoops of batter, about 2 inches apart, onto the prepared baking sheets. Press a few blackberries into each scoop. Bake in the middle of the oven for 10–12 minutes for large whoopies or 8–10 minutes for mini whoopies, until the cakes are left with a slight impression when touched with a finger.
4. Remove from the oven to a wire rack and cool completely.

TO ASSEMBLE:
Spread a generous scoop of Blackberry Cream (page 78) on the flat surface of a cooled whoopie. Drizzle with Blackberry-Geranium Sauce (page 80). Top with another whoopie and serve with more sauce.

blackberry cream

· ·

▶ Makes enough to fill about 9 large or 24 mini whoopie pies

1 cup fresh blackberries
2 tablespoons sugar
½ teaspoon pure vanilla extract
1 teaspoon fresh lemon juice
1¾ cups heavy cream

1. Put the blackberries, sugar, vanilla, and lemon juice into a bowl and toss to coat. Use the back of a fork to break up the berries a little. Let the mixture macerate for 10 minutes.

2. Whisk the cream until it just starts to thicken. Fold in the berries and chill for at least 10 minutes before using. Use on the same day as making.

blackberry-geranium sauce

▶ Makes enough to drizzle over 9 large or 24 mini whoopie pies

¼ cup sugar
3 tablespoons water
4 rose geranium leaves, rinsed and patted dry
3 cups fresh blackberries

1. Put the sugar and water into a small saucepan and heat to dissolve the sugar, but do not stir. Once the sugar has dissolved, remove the pan from the heat. Drop the geranium leaves into the sugar syrup and steep for about 10 minutes.

2. Purée half the blackberries in a food processor or blender, or crush the berries with the back of a wooden spoon. Add the geranium syrup to the purée and strain the mixture through a fine mesh sieve. Discard the blackberry seeds and geranium leaves.

3. Add the remaining whole blackberries to the sauce and stir to combine. Chill until ready to use. Best used on the same day as making but will keep in a sealed container in the fridge for up to 2 days.

NOTE:
Please note that more than one species of plant go by "geranium." *Gernanium pelargonium*, called "rose," "sweet," or "scented geranium," has edible leaves, while more common ornamental geraniums, *Geranium senecio*, are not safe to eat.

In this old-time combination of flavors, the rhubarb in the sauce is roasted rather than stewed, which intensifies its tartness, while the sweet vanilla custard filling provides the perfect foil.

rhubarb & custard whoopie pies

· ·

FILLING SUGGESTION: Vanilla Custard (Recipe for Vanilla Custard Cream on page 94; omit the cream)

DRIZZLE SUGGESTION: Roasted Rhubarb (Recipe on page 84)

► Makes about 9 large or 24 mini whoopie pies

> 2 cups plus 2 tablespoons (300 g) all-purpose flour
> 1½ teaspoons baking powder
> ¼ teaspoon salt
> 9 tablespoons (1 stick plus 1 tablespoon) unsalted butter, softened
> 1 cup (200 g) sugar
> 2 large eggs
> 1 teaspoon pure vanilla extract
> Scraped seeds of ½ vanilla pod
> ⅔ cup buttermilk
> 1 teaspoon baking soda

1. Preheat the oven to 350°F. Line two baking sheets with parchment paper.
2. In a bowl, sift together the flour and baking powder. Stir in the salt and set aside.
3. In a separate bowl, cream together the softened butter and sugar until light and fluffy, using an electric hand mixer or a standing mixer fitted with the flat beater. Add the eggs, one at a time, and mix well. Mix in the vanilla and the seeds. Measure out the buttermilk in a liquid measuring cup and stir in the baking soda. Pour this into the butter mixture and mix well. Add the dry ingredients, mixing until just incorporated. Chill for 30 minutes.
4. Drop 18 large or 48 small scoops of batter, about 2 inches apart, onto the prepared baking sheets. Bake in the middle of the oven for 10–12 minutes for large whoopies or 8–10 minutes for mini whoopies, until the cakes are left with a slight impression when touched with a finger.
5. Remove from the oven to a wire rack and cool completely.

TO ASSEMBLE:

Spread a generous scoop of plain Vanilla Custard (page 94; cream omitted) on the flat surface of a cooled whoopie. Drizzle with Roasted Rhubarb (page 84) and top with another whoopie.

roasted rhubarb

▶ Makes enough to drizzle over 9 large or 24 mini whoopie pies

> **10 ounces rhubarb**
> **2 to 3 tablespoons sugar (adjust for the tartness of the rhubarb)**
> **1 teaspoon orange zest**
> **Scraped seeds of ½ vanilla pod**

1. Preheat the oven to 350°F.

2. Cut the rhubarb into 1½-inch lengths (if they are really fat sticks, slice them through the middle first). Arrange the rhubarb in the bottom of a nonreactive roasting dish and sprinkle with the sugar. Add the orange zest and the vanilla seeds.

3. Cover the rhubarb with aluminum foil and roast in the oven for 30 minutes.

4. Remove the foil and roast for 20 minutes more, to reduce the sauce that will have formed. Leave to cool before using. The rhubarb will keep in a sealed container in the fridge for up to 2 weeks.

Banana cream pie is an American institution. Turning it into a whoopie pie seems only natural.

banana cream whoopie pies

FILLING SUGGESTION: Vanilla Custard Cream (Recipe on page 94)
DRIZZLE SUGGESTION: Chocolate Sauce and Salty Caramel Sauce (Recipes on pages 90 and 93)
SPRINKLE SUGGESTION: Chocolate Shavings (Recipe on page 90)
► Makes about 9 large or 24 small whoopie pies

> 2 cups (280 g) all-purpose flour
> ½ teaspoon baking powder
> ½ teaspoon baking soda
> ¼ teaspoon salt
> 1 large banana, plus 2 more for serving
> ⅔ cup crème fraîche
> 9 tablespoons (1 stick plus 1 tablespoon) unsalted butter, softened
> ½ cup (100 g) sugar
> ½ cup (100 g) light brown sugar
> 1 large egg

1. Preheat the oven to 350°F. Line two baking sheets with parchment paper.
2. In a bowl, sift together the flour, baking powder, and baking soda. Stir in the salt and set aside. In a separate bowl, mash up one banana, stir in the crème fraîche, and set aside.
3. In another bowl, cream the butter and sugars until light and fluffy with an electric hand mixer or in a standing mixer fitted with the flat beater. Add the egg and mix well. Add the banana mixture and beat until combined. Add the dry ingredients until just mixed. Chill for 30 minutes.
4. Drop 18 large or 48 small scoops of batter, about 2 inches apart, onto the prepared baking sheets. Bake in the middle of the oven for 10–12 minutes for large whoopies or 8–10 minutes for mini whoopies.
5. Remove from the oven to a wire rack and cool completely.

TO ASSEMBLE:
Spread a cooled whoopie with Chocolate Sauce (page 90). Add a generous scoop of Vanilla Custard Cream (page 94) and some sliced banana. Drizzle with Salty Caramel Sauce (page 93). Top with another whoopie, more sauce, and sprinkle with Chocolate Shavings (page 90).

chocolate sauce & shavings

· ·

FOR THE SAUCE
   1 cup heavy cream
   4 ounces dark chocolate, chopped

FOR THE SHAVINGS
   4- to 8-ounce dark chocolate bar (the thicker the bar, the better the results)

1. To make the sauce, heat the cream in a small saucepan. Just before it starts to boil, remove the pan from the heat. Drop the chopped chocolate into the pan and stir to melt. Let the sauce cool for 15 minutes before using. Once cool, it will keep in a sealed container in the fridge for up to 5 days.

2. For the chocolate shavings, leave the chocolate bar in a warmish place in your kitchen or warm the bar slightly by holding it (still wrapped) between your hands for a few moments. Use a sharp vegetable peeler to shave the chocolate bar at a slight angle. You can shave the chocolate directly onto your whoopie pies or into a container and store the shavings in the freezer for up to 3 weeks.

3. When taking the defrosted shavings from their container, use a spoon as the warmth of your hands can easily melt the delicate shavings.

salty caramel sauce

· ·

▶ Makes enough to fill about 9 large or 24 mini whoopie pies

2 tablespoons cold water
½ cup (100 g) sugar
½ cup heavy cream
1½ tablespoons unsalted butter
Pinch of sea salt

1. Put the water in a heavy-bottomed saucepan. Add the sugar and heat gently to dissolve, swirling the contents around without stirring. Once the sugar has dissolved, turn the heat up to high and bring to a boil. Cook until the caramel is dark, then whisk in the cream, taking care not to splash. Add the butter and salt and whisk until smooth.

2. Let the sauce cool before using. Will keep in a sealed container in the fridge for 1 week.

vanilla custard cream

. . . .

▶ Makes enough to fill about 9 large or 24 mini whoopie pies

Pinch of salt
¼ cup (50 g) sugar
1 tablespoon cornstarch
1 large egg
1 cup whole milk
½ vanilla pod, seeds scraped
1½ tablespoons unsalted butter, cut into pieces
3 tablespoons heavy cream (omit for a plain vanilla custard)

1. In a bowl, mix together the salt, sugar, and cornstarch. Whisk in the egg to make a paste.

2. In a saucepan, heat the milk, and vanilla until the mixture starts to froth but does not boil. Remove from the heat.

3. Slowly pour half of the hot milk into the egg mixture, whisking as you go.

4. Now pour the egg mixture back into the pan of hot milk and whisk.

5. Return to the heat, whisking until the custard thickens.

6. Strain the custard through a fine mesh sieve into a heatproof bowl. As it starts to cool, stir in the butter.

7. Press plastic wrap down on the surface of the custard. Leave to cool for 20 minutes, then chill for 2 hours. Will keep for 5 days in a sealed container in the fridge. Before using, whip the cream and fold into the chilled custard.

frozen & chilled whoopie pies

Ice cream sandwiches are one of the best things in life! The whoopie pie as an ice cream sandwich is a natural evolution. I prefer a soft, cakey ice cream sandwich to a wafery one. These sandwiches can be made using any of the cakes in this book and your favorite ice cream (homemade or store-bought). I have included two quick and easy ice cream recipes that don't require you to have an ice cream machine, so anyone can make them.

All the flavor of an oatmeal cookie but with a soft whoopie texture, this makes a great treat when sandwiched with vanilla ice cream and frozen, or served at room temperature with strawberry buttercream.

oatmeal cookie whoopie pies

FILLING SUGGESTION: Good-quality vanilla ice cream or Strawberry Buttercream (Recipe on page 16)
▶ Makes 24 bite-sized ice cream whoopie sandwiches

1⅓ cups (180 g) all-purpose flour
1 teaspoon baking soda
1 teaspoon cinnamon
Pinch of salt
2 sticks (1 cup) unsalted butter, softened
1 cup (200 g) light brown sugar
2 large eggs
1 teaspoon pure vanilla extract
2 cups rolled oats
½ cup raisins (optional)
Good-quality vanilla ice cream, for the filling

1. Preheat the oven to 350°F. Line two baking sheets with parchment paper.
2. In a bowl, sift together the flour, baking soda and cinnamon. Stir in the salt and set aside.
3. In a separate bowl, cream together the butter and light brown sugar until light and fluffy, using an electric hand mixer or a standing mixer fitted with the flat beater. Add the eggs, one at a time, and then the vanilla, mixing well. Add the dry ingredients and mix until combined. Add the oats and raisins and mix until incorporated. Chill for 30 minutes
4. Drop 48 small scoops of batter, about 2 inches apart, onto the prepared baking sheets. Bake in the middle of the oven for 8–10 minutes, until the cakes are left with a slight impression when touched with a finger.
5. Remove from the oven to a wire rack and cool completely.

TO ASSEMBLE:
Spread a generous scoop of slightly softened vanilla ice cream on the flat surface of a cooled whoopie. Top with another whoopie, gently press together and place in the freezer for at least 15 minutes.

The Key limes used in the authentic American pie recipe are not readily available everywhere, but you can use any variety of fresh lime juice in this whoopie pie variation.

key lime whoopie pies

• •

FILLING SUGGESTION: Frozen Key Lime Cream (Recipe on page 102)
▶ Makes about 9 large or 24 mini whoopie pies

>   **2 cups plus 2 tablespoons (300 g) all-purpose flour**
>   **1 teaspoon baking powder**
>   **1 teaspoon baking soda**
>   **¼ teaspoon salt**
>   **9 tablespoons (1 stick plus 1 tablespoon) unsalted butter, softened**
>   **1 cup (200 g) sugar**
>   **1 large egg**
>   **6 tablespoons whole milk**
>   **3 tablespoons fresh lime juice**
>   **Zest of 2 or 3 limes**

   1. Preheat the oven to 350°F. Line two baking sheets with parchment paper.
   2. In a bowl, sift together the flour, baking powder, and baking soda. Stir in the salt and set aside.
   3. In a separate bowl, cream together the softened butter and the sugar until light and fluffy, using an electric hand mixer or a standing mixer fitted with the flat beater. Add the egg and mix well. In a liquid measuring cup, combine the milk and lime juice. Pour half of this liquid into the butter mixture and mix well. Add half of the dry ingredients, mixing until just incorporated, then pour in the remaining milk-lime liquid and mix to combine. Add the rest of the dry ingredients and mix just until incorporated. Finally, fold in the lime zest. Chill for 30 minutes.
   4. Drop 18 large or 48 small scoops of batter, about 2 inches apart, onto the prepared baking sheets. Bake in the middle of the oven for 10–12 minutes for large whoopies or 8–10 minutes for mini whoopies, until the cakes are left with a slight impression when touched with a finger.
   5. Remove from the oven to a wire rack and cool completely.

TO ASSEMBLE:
Sandwich together the whoopie cakes with discs of Frozen Key Lime Cream (page 102) and then place in the freezer for at least 15 minutes before serving.

frozen key lime cream

▶ Makes enough to fill about 9 large or 24 mini whoopie pies

6 large egg yolks
¼ cup (50 g) sugar
One 14-ounce can sweetened condensed milk
2 tablespoons grated lime zest
Freshly squeezed juice of 5 limes

1. Line the cups of a large or mini muffin tin with plastic wrap and place in the freezer.

2. Beat the egg yolks and sugar on high speed in the bowl of a standing mixer fitted with a whisk for 5 minutes, until thickened. Now, with the mixer on medium speed, add the condensed milk, lime zest, and lime juice.

3. Pour or scoop the mixture into the prepared muffin tin and smooth the tops with a palette knife or an offset spatula. Freeze overnight.

This mint chip ice cream sandwich never fails to cheer up friends. It takes a little preparation, but the result is worth it.

chocolate mint whoopie pies

FILLING SUGGESTION: Frozen Mint Chip Cream (Recipe on page 106)
▶ Makes about 9 large or 24 mini whoopie pies

1¼ cups (175 g) all-purpose flour
¾ cup (100 g) unsweetened cocoa powder
1½ teaspoons baking soda
½ teaspoon baking powder
½ teaspoon salt
9 tablespoons (1 stick plus 1 tablespoon) unsalted butter, softened
1 cup (200 g) sugar
1 large egg
1 cup buttermilk
1 teaspoon peppermint extract

1. Preheat the oven to 350°F. Line two baking sheets with parchment paper.
2. In a bowl, sift together the flour, cocoa powder, baking soda, and baking powder. Stir in the salt and set aside.
3. In a separate bowl, cream together the softened butter and sugar until light and fluffy, using an electric hand mixer or a standing mixer fitted with the flat beater. Add the egg and mix well. Add the buttermilk and peppermint and beat until well combined. Slowly add the dry ingredients in two batches, mixing until just incorporated. Chill for 30 minutes.
4. Drop 18 large or 48 small scoops of batter, about 2 inches apart, onto the prepared baking sheets. Bake in the middle of the oven for 10–12 minutes for large whoopies or 8–10 minutes for mini whoopies, until the cakes are left with a slight impression when touched with a finger.
5. Remove from the oven to a wire rack and cool completely.

TO ASSEMBLE:
Use a round cookie cutter that's the same size as the cups in your muffin tins to trim down the whoopies to the same size as the discs of Frozen Mint Chip Cream (page 106). Sandwich together the whoopies with the frozen discs and place in the freezer for at least 15 minutes.

frozen mint chip cream

▶ Makes enough filling for about about 9 large or 24 mini whoopie pies

¾ cup heavy cream
Half of a 14-ounce can sweetened condensed milk
½ teaspoon peppermint oil
2 ounces dark chocolate

1. Line the cups of a large or mini muffin tin with plastic wrap and place in the freezer.

2. Beat the heavy cream to very soft peaks. Whisk in the sweetened condensed milk until smooth. Fold in the peppermint oil, and taste. Add a little more peppermint if you like it slightly stronger. Remember that when the mixture is frozen, the flavors will be more subtle. Use a vegetable peeler or Microplane zester to shave thin bits of chocolate into the cream mixture. Fold together and scoop into the prepared tins. Smooth the tops and freeze overnight.

holiday
whoopie pies

Christmas cake was a revelation when I moved to London from California, having always thought that fruitcake was sort of a cruel joke. It's now something I look forward to every year and can't get enough of. When made right, it is magnificent. So I just had to make a Christmas cake whoopie pie. Easter and Halloween are my two favorite holidays so they, too, have their own festive whoopie pies.

These are adorable with a spicy cream in the middle and a pretty glaze on top. Inverted gold paper cases and edible gold balls add an extra festive touch.

christmas cake whoopie pies

FILLING SUGGESTION: Brown Sugar Spice Buttercream (Recipe on page 112)
GLAZE SUGGESTION: Plain Icing (Recipe on page 50)
▶ Makes about 9 large or 24 mini whoopie pies

> 1 tablespoon brandy
> Zest and juice of ½ orange
> ¼ cup currants
> ¼ cup candied citrus peel, chopped
> 2 cups plus 2 tablespoons (300 g) all-purpose flour
> 6 tablespoons cornstarch
> 1½ teaspoons baking soda
> ½ teaspoon allspice
> ¼ teaspoon cloves
> ½ teaspoon salt
> 9 tablespoons (1 stick plus 1 tablespoon) unsalted butter, softened
> 1 cup (200 g) dark brown sugar
> 1 large egg
> ⅔ cup buttermilk
> ½ cup ground almonds

1. Preheat the oven to 350°F. Line two baking sheets with parchment paper.
2. In a bowl, combine the brandy, orange zest and juice, currants, and candied peel. Soak overnight or for at least 2 hours.
3. In another bowl, sift together the flours, baking soda, spices, and salt. In a separate bowl, cream the butter and sugar together until light and fluffy. Add the egg and mix well. Add the buttermilk and gently stir in the prepared fruit and ground almonds. Slowly add the dry ingredients, mixing until just incorporated. Chill for 30 minutes.
4. Drop 18 large or 48 small scoops of batter, about 2 inches apart, onto the prepared baking sheets. Bake in the middle of the oven for 10–12 minutes for large whoopies or 8–10 minutes for mini whoopies.
5. Remove from the oven to a wire rack and cool completely.

TO ASSEMBLE:
Spread a generous scoop of Brown Sugar Spice Buttercream (page 112) on a cooled cake. Top with another cake and drizzle with Plain Icing (page 50). Decorate with a gold ball and gold paper case.

brown sugar spice buttercream

▷ Makes enough to fill about 9 large or 24 mini whoopie pies

> 2 sticks (1 cup) unsalted butter, softened
> 3 large egg whites
> ½ cup (100 g) dark brown sugar
> 1 tablespoon golden syrup
> ¼ teaspoon allspice

1. Beat the butter until fluffy, using an electric hand mixer or a standing mixer fitted with the flat beater. In the bowl of a standing mixer, combine the egg whites with the sugar, golden syrup, and allspice. Place over a saucepan of barely simmering water and whisk continuously by hand until the sugar has dissolved and the mixture is frothy and slightly opaque (10–15 minutes).

2. Transfer the bowl of egg whites to the standing mixer and whisk until fluffy and cooled (about 10 minutes). Once cool, start adding the creamed butter in small batches, whisking well after each addition. The mixture will curdle but then come back together again. Switch to the flat beater and beat for 3 minutes more. If not using right away, store in a sealed container in the fridge for up to 5 days. Bring to room temperature and beat with a flat beater before using.

These are hilarious to make and were inspired by one of my baking icons, Martha Stewart. Get creative—it's scary what you're capable of. You can use any sweets you like to decorate the top.

spooky halloween whoopie pies

- -

▶ Makes 4 large and 13 mini whoopie pies

Vanilla Whoopie Pies (Recipe for Easter Egg Whoopie Pies on page 119)
Multicolored Buttercreams (Recipe on page 120), using black and green food coloring
Licorice Allsorts
Black licorice laces
Colored and chocolate-covered buttons
Red Fruit Roll-Ups
Mini marshmallows

1. Bake a combination of large and mini whoopie pies according to the instructions on page 119. For a mix of sizes, use 8 large scoops and 26 small scoops of batter, and bake for 10 minutes. This will make 4 large and 13 mini whoopies—but do not assemble them yet.

2. Now follow the recipe for Multicolored Buttercreams on page 120. Separate the buttercream into three bowls. Color one black (which turns out tombstone grey), one green (like slime), and leave the third a ghostly white.

3. Spread or pipe a generous scoop of one of the colored buttercreams onto the surface of a cooled cake. Top with another cake. Now use offset spatula to spread the various colors of buttercream on the tops of the pies.

4. Cut the candies into shapes with kitchen scissors. Licorice laces or round Licorice Allsorts, thinly snipped, make great eyeballs. Fruit leather makes a perfect tongue, and mini marshmallows make good teeth.

5. Stick the sweets however you like into the freshly applied icing so that they stay put.

These festive whoopie pies capture the pastel colors of the hand-dyed Easter eggs many families make each year and then hide in their backyards for the annual Easter egg hunt.

easter egg whoopie pies

. . . .

FILLING SUGGESTION: Multicolored Buttercreams (Recipe on page 120)
▶ Makes 24 mini whoopie pies

2 cups (280 g) all-purpose flour
¼ teaspoon baking powder
¼ teaspoon baking soda
Pinch of salt
10½ tablespoons (1 stick plus 2½ tablespoons) unsalted butter, softened
½ cup plus 2 tablespoons (125 g) sugar
1 large egg
1 large egg yolk
6 tablespoons whole milk
1 teaspoon pure vanilla extract

1. Preheat the oven to 350°F. Line two baking sheets with parchment paper.
2. In a bowl, sift together the flour, baking powder, and baking soda. Stir in the salt and set aside.
3. In a separate bowl, cream the softened butter and sugar together until light and fluffy, using an electric hand mixer or a standing mixer fitted with the flat beater. Add the egg and the egg yolk and mix well. Add the milk and vanilla to the butter mixture. Slowly add the dry ingredients, mixing until just incorporated. Chill for 30 minutes.
4. Drop 48 small scoops of batter, about 2 inches apart, onto the prepared baking sheets. Bake in the middle of the oven for 8–10 minutes, until the cakes are left with a slight impression when touched with a finger.
5. Remove from the oven to a wire rack and cool completely.

TO ASSEMBLE:
Spread or pipe a generous scoop of one of the Multicolored Buttercreams (page 120) onto the flat surface of a cooled cake. Top with another cake and decorate the sides with rainbow edible sprinkles if desired. Place the assembled whoopie pies in colorful paper cases in little boxes, baskets, or pretty bowls.

multicolored buttercreams

· ·

▶ Makes enough to fill 24 mini whoopie pies

>2 sticks (1 cup) unsalted butter, softened
>3 large egg whites
>½ cup (100 g) sugar
>1 tablespoon golden syrup
>1 teaspoon pure vanilla extract
>Selection of food colorings

1. In a bowl, beat the butter until fluffy. In the bowl of a standing mixer, combine the egg whites with the sugar and golden syrup. Place over a saucepan of barely simmering water and whisk by hand until the sugar has dissolved and the mixture is frothy and slightly opaque (10–15 minutes). Transfer the bowl to the mixer, add the vanilla, and whisk until fluffy and cooled (about 10 minutes). Once cool, start adding the creamed butter in small batches, whisking well after each addition. Switch to the flat beater and beat for 3 minutes more.

2. Separate the mixture into three or four bowls and add different food colorings of your choice to each bowl. If not using right away, store in separate sealed containers in the fridge for up to 5 days. Bring to room temperature and beat with a flat beater before using.

a few other sweet treats

· ·

In the spirit of all the whoopie pies thus far presented, here are
some other sweet "sandwiches"—peanut butter sandwich cookies,
s'mores, and easy chocolate macaroons—plus just a few other
recipes I thought you absolutely wouldn't want to live without!

These chocolaty marshmallow sandwiches get their name from the pleas of children begging for some more, or s'more.

s'mores

· ·

Bamboo skewers, or roasting sticks cut from a tree branch
Large marshmallows, from a packet
Your favorite milk or dark chocolate bar, broken into squares
Graham crackers

1. Use bamboo skewers or roasting sticks to toast the marshmallows over a campfire or gas-burner flame.

2. To assemble the s'mores, put a square of chocolate on a cracker, place the hot marshmallow on top, and cover with another cracker, holding down the sandwich and pulling out the skewer or stick.

Peanut butter cookies taste even better when sandwiched with a peanut butter cream. These cookies have a little crunch to them, which is a nice contrast in texture to the lighter-than-air filling.

peanut butter sandwich cookies

FILLING SUGGESTION: Peanut Butter Cream (Recipe on page 128)
▶ Makes 24 sandwich cookies

1⅓ cups (180 g) all-purpose flour
¾ teaspoon baking soda
Pinch of salt
2 sticks (1 cup) unsalted butter, softened
1 cup (200 g) light brown sugar
1 large egg
1 large egg yolk
¾ cup crunchy peanut butter
1 teaspoon pure vanilla extract
¼ cup roasted salted peanuts

1. Preheat the oven to 350°F. Line two baking sheets with parchment paper.
2. In a bowl, sift together the flour and baking soda. Stir in the salt and set aside.
3. In a separate bowl, cream together the softened butter and the sugar until light and fluffy, using an electric hand mixer or a standing mixer fitted with the flat beater. Add the egg and the egg yolk and mix well. Add the peanut butter and vanilla to the butter mixture and mix well. Slowly add the dry ingredients, mixing until just incorporated. Chill for about 1 hour.
4. Drop 48 small scoops of batter, about 2 inches apart, onto the prepared baking sheets. Press half a peanut (flat-side up) into each ball of dough. Bake in the middle of the oven for 15–18 minutes or until set and slightly golden.
5. Remove from the oven to a wire rack and cool completely.

TO ASSEMBLE:
Spread a generous scoop of Peanut Butter Cream (page 128) on the flat side of a cooled peanut butter cookie. Top with another cookie, and serve.

peanut butter cream

- Makes enough to fill 24 peanut butter sandwich cookies

> 2 sticks (1 cup) unsalted butter, softened
> 1 cup crunchy peanut butter
> 2⅔ cups (300 g) confectioners' sugar
> ¼ teaspoon pure vanilla extract

1. In a bowl, cream the softened butter, peanut butter, and sugar together until light and fluffy, using an electric hand mixer or a standing mixer fitted with the flat beater. Whip until light and fluffy and pale in color. Add the vanilla and whip to mix.

2. Chill until ready to use. Will keep in a sealed container in the fridge for 1 week. (You can also use this peanut butter cream filling in a chocolate whoopie pie, for a delicious, super-rich snack.)

This is a simple version of the chocolate macaroons that I learned to make at Pierre Hermé's pastry school in Paris. Pierre is a genius, and his pastries are the best in the world.

easy chocolate macaroons

FILLING SUGGESTION: Chocolate-Caramel Ganache (Recipe on page 132)
▶ Makes 20 macaroon sandwiches

> 1 cup (100 g) confectioners' sugar, plus an extra 2 tablespoons
> 1/3 cup unsweetened cocoa powder
> 1 cup ground almonds
> 2 large egg whites

1. Preheat the oven to 400°F. Line two baking sheets with parchment paper.
2. In the bowl of a food processor, blend the ½ cup confectioners' sugar with the cocoa powder and ground almonds for about 3 minutes. Sift into a large bowl and set aside.
3. In a separate bowl, whisk the egg whites with the 2 tablespoons confectioners' sugar until billowy peaks form and the mixture is smooth and glossy, but not dry. Fold half of the dry ingredients into the egg whites and then fold in the remainder. Transfer the mixture to a piping bag fitted with a ¼-inch tip.

   Create a template by tracing 20 small circles about 2 inches apart on a sheet of paper and placing it underneath the parchment paper on one of the prepared baking sheets (so that you can use the template again). Pipe 20 small rounds of batter onto the parchment paper on the first baking sheet, then remove the template, place it under the parchment paper on the next baking sheet, and repeat. Remember to remove the template.
4. Tap the sheets on your work surface to release any air in the macaroons. Leave to dry out for 20 minutes. Place in the 400°F oven and immediately turn the oven down to 350°F. Bake for 2 minutes, then reduce the oven temperature to 325°F and bake for 2 minutes more. Reduce the oven temperature to 275°F and bake for a further 4 minutes. (Total baking time is 8 minutes.)
5. Remove from the oven to a wire rack and cool completely.

TO ASSEMBLE:
Spread a generous scoop of Chocolate-Caramel Ganache (page 132) on the flat surface of a cooled macaroon. Top with another macaroon, and serve.

chocolate–caramel ganache

> ▶ Makes enough to fill about 20 macaroons

6 ounces dark chocolate, finely chopped
2 tablespoons cold water
½ cup (100 g) sugar
½ cup heavy cream
1½ tablespoons unsalted butter
Pinch of sea salt

1. Place the chocolate in a large, heatproof bowl and set aside.

2. Put the water in a heavy-bottomed saucepan. Add the sugar and heat gently to dissolve, swirling the contents around without stirring. Once the sugar has dissolved, turn the heat up to high and bring to a boil. Cook until the caramel is dark. Whisk in the cream, taking care not to splash. Add the butter and salt and whisk until smooth.

3. Pour the caramel over the chopped chocolate and whisk gently until smooth and melted. Allow to set at room temperature for 2 hours until it is of a spreadable consistency. Will keep in a sealed container in the fridge for 1 week.

This recipe came to me from one of my dearest friends, Lazuli Whitt, courtesy of her mother Barbara. When Lazuli first made this cobbler for us, my husband said it was the best dessert he had ever eaten. Ahem . . .

prize peach cobbler

▶ Serves 6

¾ cup (100 g) all-purpose flour
2 teaspoons baking powder
Pinch of salt
½ cup (100 g) sugar, plus an extra ½ cup
⅔ cup whole milk
7 tablespoons unsalted butter, melted and cooled slightly
5–6 ripe peaches

1. Preheat the oven to 375°F. Line two baking sheets with parchment paper.
2. In a bowl, sift together the flour and baking powder. Stir in the salt and ¼ cup sugar and then slowly whisk in the milk. Now whisk in the melted butter in a steady stream to form a pancake-like batter, then set aside.
3. Bring a saucepan of water to the boil and set up a bowl filled with iced water and a slotted spoon (or spider) next to the stovetop. Once the water in the pan is boiling, gently drop in the peaches (you may need to do this in two batches). Blanch the peaches for a minute only and then remove them with a slotted spoon, submerging them in the ice water bath to stop them from cooking. Slip off the skins and then quarter and core the peaches and remove the stones. You may want to slice them again if the peaches are large. Pour the extra ¼ cup sugar into a bowl, then toss the quartered peaches in the sugar and transfer to a large gratin dish.
4. Pour the batter over the peaches and bake in the middle of the oven for about 1 hour. The cobbler is ready when it bubbles and turns golden and a skewer inserted comes out clean.

Blondies have the texture and richness of brownies, but without the chocolate—hence the name. I have snuck in some chunks of milk chocolate here, but the body of the blondie tastes like butterscotch.

butterscotch blondies

▶ Makes about 16 blondies

> 3 sticks (1½ cups) plus 1 tablespoon unsalted butter, softened
> 2⅓ cups (320 g) all-purpose flour
> 1½ teaspoons baking powder
> 1½ teaspoons sea salt
> 3 large eggs
> 2 cups (400 g) dark brown sugar
> 2 teaspoons pure vanilla extract
> 8-ounce milk chocolate bar with toffee, chopped into small pieces

1. Preheat the oven to 325°F. Butter and line a 9-inch-square cake pan with parchment paper so that it comes up the sides of the pan.
2. Gently melt the butter in a heatproof bowl over a pan of barely simmering water. Set aside to cool slightly.
3. In another bowl, sift together the flour and baking powder, then stir in the salt and set aside. In a separate bowl, whisk together the eggs, sugar, and vanilla until frothy, then whisk in the melted butter. Fold in the dry ingredients until just mixed, then fold in the chocolate pieces. Pour into your prepared baking pan.
4. Bake in the middle of the oven for about 35 minutes. A skewer inserted should come out ever so slightly gooey. Leave to cool completely in the baking pan, then cut into smallish squares. These are rich!

A great idea for a dessert is to bake some brownies, dollop on some vanilla ice cream, and top with chocolate sauce, preserved cherries, and toasted flaked almonds.

brownie sundae

▶ Makes about 6–12 brownies

10 ounces dark chocolate, chopped
10½ tablespoons (1 stick plus 2½ tablespoons) unsalted butter
3 large eggs
¾ cup (150 g) dark brown sugar
¼ cup (50 g) sugar
½ teaspoon sea salt
2 teaspoons pure vanilla extract
¾ cup (100 g) all-purpose flour

FOR THE TOPPING
½ cup sliced almonds
Good-quality vanilla ice cream
Good-quality cherries in syrup
Chocolate Sauce (Recipe on page 90)

1. Preheat the oven to 325°F. Butter and line a 9-inch-square cake pan with parchment paper so that it comes up the sides of the tin.
2. Place the chocolate and butter in a heatproof bowl and melt over a pan of barely simmering water. In another bowl, whisk the eggs, sugars, salt, and vanilla until frothy, then whisk in the melted chocolate. Fold in the flour until just mixed, then pour the batter into your prepared baking pan.
3. Bake in the middle of the oven for about 25 minutes. These brownies are better when slightly underdone. A skewer inserted should come out a little wet. Leave to cool completely in the baking pan, then cut into generous-sized squares.
4. For the topping, toast the sliced almonds lightly in the oven (these will keep for up to a week in a sealed container).
5. To serve, place a brownie in each serving bowl, add a scoop of vanilla ice cream, then drizzle with chocolate sauce and top with a few cherries. Finish with a sprinkling of toasted sliced almonds.

acknowledgments

A very special thanks to Adriana (Dri) Nascimento for giving so much time and dedication to Violet, for being such a gifted baker, and for making all of us laugh all the time.

Huge thanks to the Violet girls—Samantha Dixon, Echo Hopkins, Alexandra Postans, Mariana Kazarnovsky, Meridith Bradley, Julie Solovyeva, and Jane Potthast—for everything they do every day at Violet. Thanks to our interns, Andrew Findley and Fiona Wymes, who won the hearts of us all. We miss you! Thanks to Jack Coleman for his exquisite coffee and to Leila McAllister for sourcing our beautiful produce.

Thank you to my publisher Matthew Lore for believing in this project enough to bring it to America, to my British editor Rowan Yapp at Random House for her trust and belief and for giving me the freedom to make this book look the way I wanted, to Elisabeth Ptak and Jan Bowmer for their fantastic edits, to Lori Galvin for the arduous task of converting the measurements from metric into cups, and to Pauline Neuwirth and Susi Oberhelman for the great design. A big thank-you to Colin "Big C" Campbell for his inspired photographs and for his unparalleled work ethic.

Thank you to Brigit Devlin and Debra Ruff for giving me my first job at the Bovine Bakery when I was only 15. Thanks to these fellow crazy cooks and collaborators: Jessica Boncutter, April Bloomfeld, Jamie Oliver, Ignacio Mattos, David Tanis, David Lindsay, Christopher Lee, Alan Tangren, Yolanda Porrata, Louis Ptak, Todd Selby, Nicole Bartolini, Lazuli Whitt, Alex Porrata, Dakota Whitney, Stevie Parle, Blanche Vaughan, and Tommi Miers.

Thank you to Alice Waters and Fanny Singer for so much love and support. I cherish our collaborations and friendship.

Finally, thanks to Damian for everything.

index